This book
was prensented
to

Kelly Holmes

by

Grandma & Papa Bill

on

July 28 2010

STORYTIME COLLECTION FOR FOUR YEAR OLDS


Printed in China


17862/0808

ISBN: 1-40375-553-1

08 09 10 11 12 CTP 10 9 8 7 6 5 4 3 2 1

storytime collection for

# FOUR YEAR OLDS

Dalmatian Press

# TABLE OF CONTENTS

# Hansel & Gretel

A Grimm Tale

Adapted by Joe Loesch
Illustrated by Kevin Menck

Once upon a time there was a boy and girl named Hansel and Gretel. They lived with their father, a poor woodcutter, in a little house beside a forest. Often the family went to bed hungry because there was not enough food to eat.

One day the woodcutter took his children into the forest to gather wood.

Hansel and Gretel laughed and played so hard that they wandered from their father and were soon lost. Their father looked for them the rest of that day. Fortunately, Hansel had many of his favorite pebbles with him, and they had fallen to the ground one by one from the holes in his pockets. The children followed the path of shiny pebbles by moonlight back to their home. Their father was very happy to see them, but warned Hansel and Gretel to stay close to home and not to wander away.

A week later, the children went to play in the forest again. They did not heed their father's warning and wandered far from home, leaving a trail of bread crumbs behind them to follow back home.

But the bread crumbs were eaten by the birds in the forest. And so, Hansel and Gretel realized they were lost.

The children became tired and very hungry as they roamed through the forest.

Suddenly, there through the trees, they saw a strange little house made of cake and candy!

They ran to the house and began eating from it furiously. There were cake shingles and candy shutters. The windows were made of sugar. The flowers were lollipops.

As they started to take a bite from the chocolate door, it opened.

Out stepped an old woman with a wart on her nose.

"Who's eating my house?" she said.

The children were startled at first, but the old lady seemed very kind.

Hansel and Gretel apologized for eating from her house.

"We haven't eaten in such a long time," they said.

The old lady took them in and fed them some good wholesome food. "This will fatten you up!" she said slyly.

It wasn't long before the old lady's kindly spirit wore off. She snarled and ordered the children to work from morning till night. She had Gretel scrubbing floors and cleaning the oven. Hansel had to repair a broken table and gather heavy wood for the stove.

"Only a witch would act this way," Gretel told Hansel.

Still, the witch fed them well. Hansel and Gretel even gained a little weight.

One night, as the witch stoked the coals in her oven, Gretel heard her cackle, "Tonight I'll have Hansel and Gretel for dinner!"

At that, Gretel sneaked up behind the witch—and pushed her into the oven!

The witch was destroyed by the flames, and the oven became so hot that the house caught fire!

As Hansel and Gretel ran to the door, they came across chests full of gems and coins of gold. They gathered as much as they could into two potato sacks, and then fled from the house. They ran until they could run no farther.

They sat beneath a tree to catch their breath. Suddenly they heard a voice call out, "Hansel! Gretel!" It was their father, who had been searching for them since the day they were lost. They ran to their father's loving embrace.

"Look, Father," Hansel exclaimed, opening a sack. "More gold than we've ever dreamed of! We'll never be poor or hungry again!"

From that day on, Hansel and Gretel lived happily ever after with their father in the little house beside the forest, and they never went wandering again.

*The End*

# Jack and the Beanstalk

Adapted by Ashley Crownover
Illustrated by David Wariner

Once upon a time there was a poor widow and her only son, Jack. Life was hard for them. At last, all Jack and his mother had left was their milking cow.

One day Jack's mother said sadly, "Jack, you must take the cow to market and sell her. We have nothing left to eat."

Jack loved his cow and didn't want to sell her, but he knew there was no other choice. So he set out early the next day for market.

On the way, Jack met a strange old man who offered him five beautiful rainbow-colored beans in exchange for the cow. “They’re magic!” the man said. Jack eagerly agreed to the trade.

Jack ran home to show his mother the wonderful beans. But when he told her what had happened, she was very angry. "Trading a cow for five worthless beans!" she said. "Now we'll starve!" She threw the beans out the window, and they both went to bed hungry.

When Jack woke the next morning, he found that an enormous beanstalk had sprung up outside the window. He quickly began to climb it, going higher and higher, until at last he reached the top.

There Jack saw an enormous castle.

A woman answered the castle door, and Jack said, "I am very hungry. Can you give me something to eat?"

"No!" said the woman. "Go away! My husband, the Giant, will eat you!"

But Jack begged, and finally the Giant's wife let him in. Just then they heard a loud thump, thump, thump.

"He's coming!" the woman cried. "Hide in the oven!"

Jack jumped into the oven.

The Giant came in shouting, “Fee, fie, fo, fum! Look out, Human, here I come! Eyes, ears, hands and feet. I smell something good to eat!”

“Nonsense,” said his wife.

The Giant sat down and called for his magic hen. “Lay!” he roared, and the hen laid a golden egg. Then the Giant dozed off.

Jack crept out of the oven, snatched up the hen, and ran away as fast as he could!

He climbed down the beanstalk and took the hen to his mother.

Jack and his mother lived happily for a long time by selling the hen's golden eggs.

But it wasn't long before Jack decided to climb the beanstalk again to seek more treasures.

He returned to the castle and knocked on the big door.

"No," said the Giant's wife when she came to the door. "The last time I fed you, you stole my husband's hen."

But Jack begged, and the Giant's wife let him in. Just then they heard a loud thump, thump, thump.

"Quick!" said the Giant's wife. "Hide in this kettle!"

The Giant came in shouting, "Fee, fie, fo, fum! Look out, Human, here I come! Eyes, ears, hands and feet. I smell something good to eat!"

"You're always saying that," his wife replied. "Come eat your supper."

After supper, the Giant got out his enchanted harp. "Play!" commanded the Giant, and the golden harp began to play all by itself.

After a while, the Giant fell asleep, snoring loudly. Jack jumped out of the kettle and grabbed the harp. The harp cried out, "Master, Master!" The Giant awoke and ran after Jack.

Jack climbed down the beanstalk with the Giant close behind him. As Jack neared the bottom he cried, "Mother! Bring the axe!"

Jack jumped to the ground and took the axe from his mother. He struck the beanstalk as hard as he could.

Down came the beanstalk—and down came the Giant!

So all ended well for Jack and his mother, if not for the Giant.

As for the magical beanstalk, it never grew again.

*The End*

# The UGLY DUCKLING

From a story by Hans Christian Andersen

Retold by Kate Sullivan Watkins

Illustrated by James Finch

One bright, sunny morning in a corner of an old farmyard, a mother duck watched proudly as her ducklings hatched from their eggs. The five new ducklings were tiny and covered with soft, yellow feathers.

But the mother duck was puzzled because one egg did not hatch. This egg was much larger than the others.

An old duck came waddling down the path and stopped to admire the new ducklings. "What's wrong with that egg?" the old duck asked.

"I don't know," the mother replied, "but for some reason, it won't hatch."

The old duck looked carefully at the egg. "Well, that's a turkey egg," she said. "Leave it alone and go teach your new babies how to swim."

"No," said the mother duck. "I've taken care of this egg for this long. I will stay with it until the duckling hatches."

The mother duck continued to sit until the large egg began to wobble and crack. Finally, out came an unusual-looking baby bird. He was covered with rough, gray feathers, and he was much bigger than the other ducklings. His feet were large and clumsy, and his neck was long and skinny.

When the other birds in the farmyard saw him, they began to squawk. “What an ugly duckling!” honked the geese. “A very strange duckling indeed!” clucked the hens. Even the turkeys laughed at the new baby.

The poor duckling really did feel ugly. He made his way to a nearby lake to hide in the tall grass. He stayed hidden all summer long.

One night, when the moon was shining brightly on the lake, the lonely duckling saw winged creatures gliding through the sky. Three magnificent swans cast graceful shadows as they flew through the night. The duckling stood still to admire them. Oh, how he longed to fly!

When winter came to the lake, the duckling grew cold, and he had trouble finding food to eat.

One morning, the duckling slipped on the ice of the frozen lake. A kind farmer found him lying helpless and scared on the ice. The farmer wrapped him in his coat and carried him back to the nice, warm barn. The duckling stayed in the barn, and the farmer took care of him for the rest of the long, harsh winter.

Spring finally arrived, and the farmer led the duckling out of the barn. The duckling had grown. Feeling stronger than ever before, he flapped his wings gently in the warm light of the sun. To his surprise, he flew right off the ground into the bright sky.

He landed near some reeds at the edge of a peaceful pond. He could hear children playing nearby on the bank, and once again he saw the lovely swans. This time they were drifting through the water.

Afraid that they might laugh at him, the ugly duckling lowered his head in shame. As he looked down at the reflection in the still water, he saw another swan that was just as splendid as the others.

After a moment, he realized he was staring at his own reflection. He was amazed at how beautiful he had become. He was not an ugly duckling! In fact, he had never been a duckling at all, but a swan in the making. He glided into the water and joined the other swans. When the children saw him, they began to shout, "Look at the new swan. He is the most splendid of them all!"

He was no longer an ugly duckling, but a graceful and beautiful swan. "I never dreamed of such happiness," he thought. And his heart almost burst with joy.

*The End*

# FABLES *for* CHILDREN

By Aesop
Illustrated by Milo Winter

## THE YOUNG CRAB AND HIS MOTHER

"Why in the world do you walk sideways like that?" said a Mother Crab to her son. "You should always walk straight forward with your toes turned out."

"Show me how to walk, Mother dear," answered the little Crab obediently. "I want to learn."

So the old Crab tried and tried to walk straight forward. But she could only walk sideways, like her son. And when she wanted to turn her toes out, she tripped and fell on her nose.

*Do not tell others how to act unless you can set a good example*

## BELLING THE CAT

The Mice once called a meeting to decide on a plan to free themselves of their enemy, the Cat. They wished to find some way of knowing when she was coming, so they would have time to run away. Indeed, something had to be done, for they lived in such constant fear of her claws that they hardly dared stir from their dens by night or day.

They discussed many plans, but none of them was thought good enough. At last a very young Mouse got up and said:

"I have a plan that seems simple, but I know it will work. All we have to do is to hang a bell about the Cat's neck. When we hear the bell ringing, we will know immediately that she is coming."

All the Mice were much surprised that they had not thought of such a plan before. But in the midst of the rejoicing over their good fortune, an old Mouse arose and said:

"I will say that the plan of the young Mouse is very good. But let me ask one question: Who will bell the Cat?"

*It is one thing to say that something should be done, but quite a different matter to do it*

# THE TOWN MOUSE AND THE COUNTRY MOUSE

A Town Mouse once visited a cousin who lived in the country. For lunch the Country Mouse served wheat stalks, roots, and acorns, with a dash of cold water for drink. The Town Mouse ate very little, nibbling a little of this and a little of that, for she did not care for this simple country food.

After the meal the friends had a long talk, or rather the Town Mouse talked about her life in the city while the Country Mouse listened. They then went to bed in a cozy nest in the hedgerow and slept in quiet and comfort until morning. In her sleep the Country Mouse dreamed she was a Town Mouse with all the fancy delights of city life that her friend had described for her. So the next day when the Town Mouse asked the Country Mouse to go home with her to the city, she gladly said yes.

When they reached the mansion in which the Town Mouse lived, they found on the table in the dining room the leftovers of a very fine banquet. There were jellies, pastries, delicious cheeses—the most tempting foods a Mouse can imagine. But just as the Country Mouse was about to nibble a dainty bit of pastry, she heard a Cat mew loudly and scratch at the door. In great fear the Mice scurried to a hiding place, where they lay quite still for a long time, hardly daring to breathe. When at last they ventured back to the feast, the door opened suddenly and in came the servants, followed by the House Dog.

The Country Mouse ran to the Town Mouse's den and grabbed her bag and umbrella.

"You may have fancy food," she said as she hurried away, "but I prefer my plain food and simple life in the country with the peace that goes with it."

*Simplicity with safety is better than plenty with fear.*

MILO WINTER

# THE LION AND THE MOUSE

A Lion lay asleep in the forest, his great head resting on his paws. A timid little Mouse came upon him unexpectedly, and in her fright and haste to get away, ran across the Lion's nose. Roused from his nap, the Lion laid his huge paw angrily on the tiny creature to kill her.

"Spare me!" begged the poor Mouse. "Please let me go, and someday I will surely repay you."

The Lion was much amused to think that a Mouse could ever help him. But he was generous and finally let the Mouse go.

Some days later, while stalking his prey in the forest, the Lion was caught in a hunter's net. Unable to free himself, he filled the forest with his angry roaring. The Mouse knew the voice and quickly found the Lion struggling in the net. Running to one of the great ropes that bound him, she gnawed it until it broke, and soon the Lion was free.

"You laughed when I said I would repay you," said the Mouse. "Now you see that even a Mouse can help a Lion."

*A kindness is never wasted*

# THE ANTS AND THE GRASSHOPPER

One bright day in late autumn a family of Ants was bustling about in the warm sunshine, drying out the grain they had stored up during the summer, when a starving Grasshopper, his fiddle under his arm, came up and humbly begged for a bite to eat.

"What!" cried the Ants in surprise. "Haven't you stored anything away for the winter? What in the world were you doing all last summer?"

"I didn't have time to store up any food," whined the Grasshopper. "I was so busy making music that before I knew it, the summer was gone."

The Ants shrugged their shoulders in disgust.

"Making music, were you?" they cried. "Very well; now dance!" And they turned their backs on the Grasshopper and went on with their work.

*There's a time for work and a time for play*

# THE MILKMAID AND HER PAIL

A Milkmaid had been out to milk the cows and was returning from the field with the milk pail balanced nicely on her head.

"This good, rich milk," she thought, "will give me plenty of cream to make butter. I will take the butter to market, and with the money I get for it I will buy a lot of eggs for hatching. How nice it will be when they are all hatched and the yard is full of fine young chicks. Then I will sell them, and with the money I'll buy a lovely new dress to wear to the fair."

As she thought of this, she tossed her head, and down fell the pail of milk to the ground. All the milk flowed out, and so did her dreams of butter and eggs and chicks and new dress.

*Do not count your chickens before they are hatched*

# THE FOX AND THE STORK

The Fox one day thought of a plan to play a trick on his friend the Stork.

"You must come and dine with me today," he said to the Stork, smiling to himself. The Stork gladly accepted the invitation and arrived in good time and with a very good appetite.

For dinner the Fox served soup. But it was set out in a very shallow dish, and all the Stork could do was to wet the very tip of his beak. Not a drop of soup could he get. But the Fox lapped it up easily with his tongue and laughed at the stork.

The hungry Stork was much displeased at the trick, but he was a calm fellow and saw no good in getting angry. Instead, not long afterward, he invited the Fox to dine with him in turn. The Fox arrived promptly at the time that had been set, and the Stork served a fish dinner that had a very delicious smell. But it was served in a tall jar with a very narrow neck. The Stork could easily get at the food with his long beak, but all the Fox could do was to lick the outside of the jar, and sniff at the delicious odor. And when the Fox lost his temper, the Stork said calmly:

*Do not play tricks on your neighbors unless you can stand the same treatment yourself*

# TWO TRAVELERS AND A BEAR

Two Men were traveling through a forest, when, all at once, a huge Bear crashed out of the brush near them.

One of the Men, thinking of his own safety, left his friend and climbed a tree.

The other, unable to fight the savage beast alone, threw himself onto the ground and lay still, as if he were dead. He had heard that a Bear will not touch a dead body.

It must have been true, for the Bear snuffed at the Man's head awhile, and then walked away.

The Man in the tree climbed down.

"It looked just as if that Bear whispered in your ear," he said. "What did he tell you?"

"He said," answered the other, "that it was not at all smart of me to have a friend who would leave me in a moment of danger!"

*True friends stick with you, even in times of trouble*

MILO WINTER

# THE GOOSE AND THE GOLDEN EGG

There was once a Countryman who had the most wonderful Goose you can imagine; for every day when he visited the nest, the Goose had laid a beautiful, glittering, golden egg.

The Countryman took the golden eggs to market to sell and soon began to get rich. But it was not long before he grew impatient with the Goose because she gave him only one golden egg each day. He was not getting rich fast enough.

Then one day, after he had finished counting his money, the idea came to him that he could get all the golden eggs at once by killing the Goose and cutting it open. But when the deed was done, not a single golden egg did he find, and his precious Goose was dead. And so he ended up with no more golden eggs.

*Be careful of wanting more and more and more — for you may end up with less.*

## THE TORTOISE AND THE HARE

A Hare was making fun of the Tortoise one day for being so slow.

"Do you ever get anywhere?" he asked with a laugh.

"Yes," replied the Tortoise, "and I get there sooner than you think. I'll run you a race and prove it."

The Hare was very amused at the idea of running a race with the Tortoise, but for the fun of it he agreed. So the Fox, who had agreed to be the judge, marked the distance and started the runners off.

The Hare was soon far out of sight. "I will make the Tortoise feel foolish for daring to race me," thought the Hare. "I'll just lie down here and take a nap until he catches up—and then I'll zip down to the finish line." And so he went to sleep.

The Tortoise meanwhile kept going slowly but steadily, and, after a time, passed the place where the Hare was sleeping. But the Hare slept on very peacefully; and when at last he did wake up, the Tortoise was near the finish line. The Hare now ran his swiftest, but he could not overtake the Tortoise in time. And the Tortoise won the race!

*Slow and steady often wins the race.*

MILES
MILO WINTER

# THE THREE BILLY GOATS GRUFF

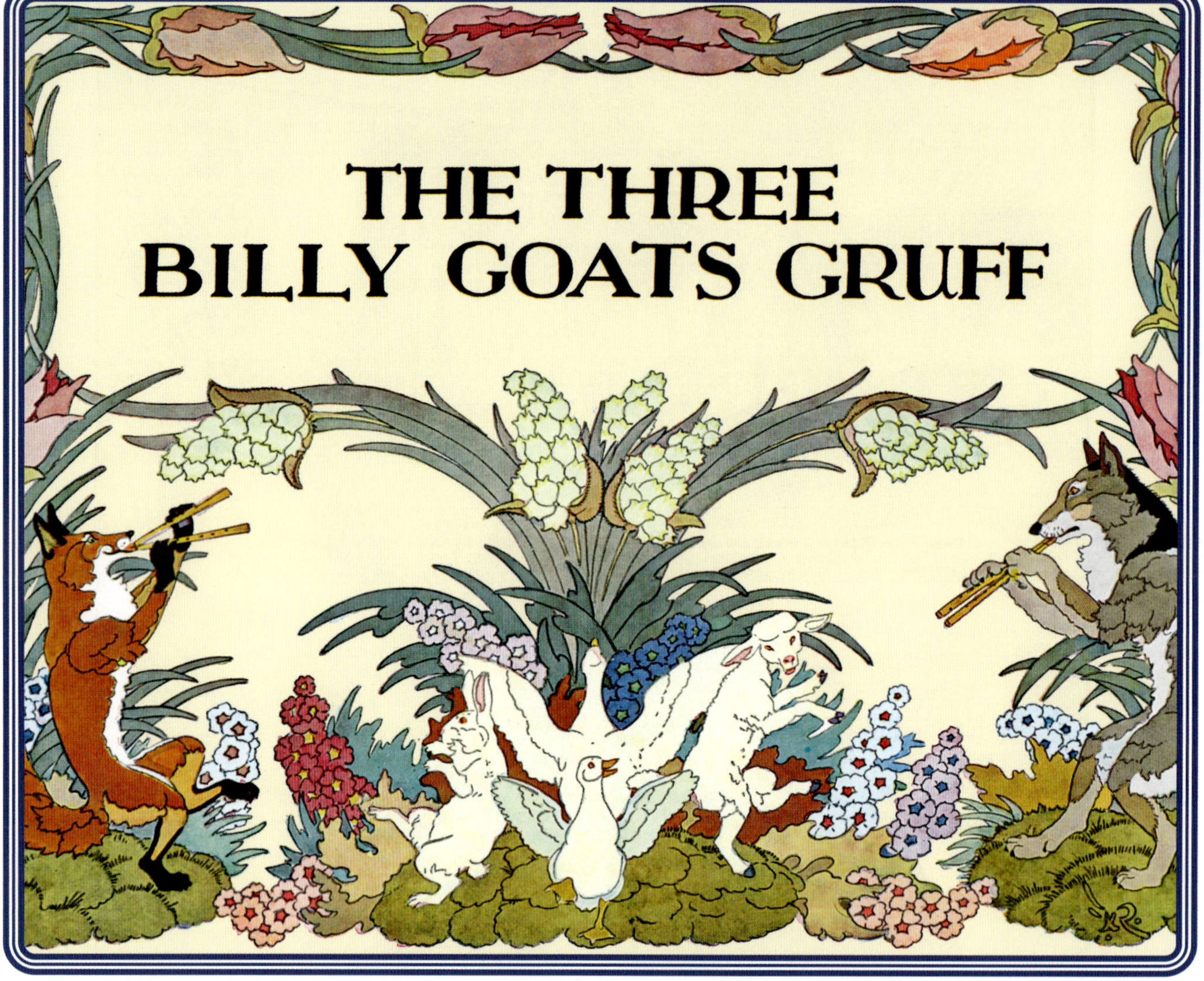

Traditional Folk Tale
Illustrated by Frederick Richardson

Once upon a time there were three billy goats, who wanted to go up to the hillside to make themselves fat, and the name of all three was Gruff.

On the way up was a bridge over a burn* they had to cross. Under the bridge lived a great ugly Troll, with eyes as big as saucers, and a nose as long as a poker.

So first of all came the youngest billy goat Gruff to cross the bridge.

"Trip, trap, trip, trap, trip, trap!" went the bridge.

"WHO'S THAT tripping over my bridge?" roared the Troll.

"Oh! It is only I, the tiniest billy goat Gruff; and I'm going up to the hillside to make myself fat," said the billy goat with such a small voice.

"Now, I'm coming to gobble you up," said the Troll.

**burn: small stream or brook*

"Oh, no! Pray don't take me. I'm too little, that I am," said the billy goat. "Wait a bit till the second billy goat Gruff comes. He's much bigger."

"Well! Be off with you," said the Troll.

A little while after came the second billy goat Gruff to cross the bridge.

"TRIP, TRAP! TRIP, TRAP! TRIP, TRAP!" went the bridge.

"WHO'S THAT tripping over my bridge?" roared the Troll.

"Oh! It's the second billy goat Gruff, and I'm going up to the hillside to make myself fat," said the billy goat, who hadn't such a small voice.

"Now, I'm coming to gobble you up," said the Troll.

"Oh, no! Don't take me. Wait a little till the big billy goat Gruff comes. He's much bigger."

"Very well! Be off with you," said the Troll.

But just then up came the big billy goat Gruff.

"TRIP, TRAP! TRIP, TRAP! TRIP, TRAP!" went the bridge, for the billy goat was so heavy that the bridge creaked and groaned under him.

"WHO'S THAT tramping over my bridge?" roared the Troll.

"IT IS I! THE BIG BILLY GOAT GRUFF!" said the billy goat, who had an ugly, hoarse voice of his own.

"Now, I'm coming to gobble you up!" roared the Troll.

"Well, come along! I've got two spears,
And I'll poke your nose and pierce your ears;
I've got besides two curling-stones,*
And I'll bruise your body and rattle your bones."

That was what the big billy goat said. And he flew at the Troll, and tossed him out into the burn, and after that he went up to the hillside.

**curling-stones: heavy stones used in the ice-sport called curling. In this case, he means his big, heavy hooves.*

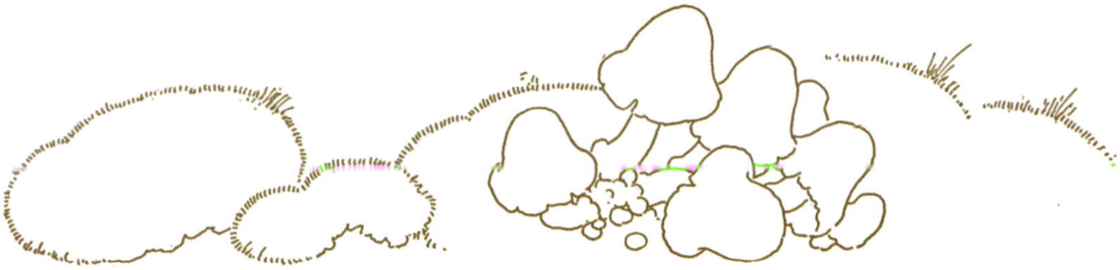

There the billy goats got so fat they were scarcely able to walk home again; and if the fat hasn't fallen off them—why, they're still fat. And so:

Snip, snap, snout!
This tale's told out.

*The End*

Traditional Folk Tale
Illustrated by Frederick Richardson

Long, long ago an old hen and her one little chicken went into the woods. The little chicken was named Tuppens. Scratch, scratch, they were busy all day among the leaves finding seeds to eat.

"Do not eat the big seeds," said the old hen to Little Tuppens, "for they will make you cough."

But by and by Little Tuppens found a big seed and ate it. Then Little Tuppens began to cough. The old hen was frightened at this and ran to the spring.

She said:

"Please, spring, give me some water.
Little Tuppens is coughing."

The spring said:

"Get me a cup and then
I will give you some water."

The old hen ran to the oak tree and said:

"Please, oak tree, give me a cup;
Then the spring will give me some water.
Little Tuppens is coughing."

The oak tree said:

"Shake me. Then I will give you a cup."

The old hen ran to a little boy and said:

"Please, little boy, shake the oak tree;
Then the oak tree will give me a cup,
And the spring will give me some water.
Little Tuppens is coughing."

The little boy said:

"Give me some shoes. Then I can shake
the oak tree for you."

The old hen ran to the shoemaker and said:

"Please, good shoemaker,
give me some shoes for the little boy;
Then the little boy will shake the oak tree,
And the oak tree will give me a cup,
And the spring will give me some water.
Little Tuppens is coughing."

The shoemaker said:

"Get me some leather and then
I will make some shoes for the little boy."

The old hen ran to the cow and said:

"Please, cow, give me some leather;
Then the shoemaker will make
shoes for the little boy,
And the little boy will shake the oak tree,
And the oak tree will give me a cup,
And the spring will give me some water.
Little Tuppens is coughing."

The cow said:

"Get me some corn and then
I will give you some leather."

The old hen ran to the farmer and said:

"Please, farmer, give me corn for the cow;
Then the cow will give me some
leather for the shoemaker,
And the shoemaker will make
shoes for the little boy,
And the little boy will shake the oak tree,
And the oak tree will give me a cup,
And the spring will give me some water.
Little Tuppens is coughing."

The farmer said:

"Get me a plow and then I can give
you some corn."

The old hen ran to the blacksmith and said:

"Please, good blacksmith, give me a plow for
the farmer;
Then the farmer will give me some
corn for the cow,
And the cow will give me some
leather for the shoemaker,
And the shoemaker will give me
some shoes for the little boy,
And the little boy will shake the oak tree,
And the oak tree will give me a cup,
And the spring will give me some water.
Little Tuppens is coughing."

The blacksmith said:

"Get me some iron and then I can give
you a plow."

The old hen ran to the dwarfs and asked for iron for the blacksmith.

When she had told her story about Little Tuppens to the dwarfs, they wanted to help. They went into their cave and brought out some iron for the blacksmith.

Then the blacksmith made a plow for the farmer,
And the farmer gave some corn for the cow,
And the cow gave some leather for the shoemaker,
And the shoemaker made some shoes for the little boy,
And the little boy shook the oak tree,
And the oak tree gave a cup,
And the spring gave some water,
And the old hen gave the water to Little Tuppens,

And Little Tuppens
stopped coughing.

*The End*

# THE VELVETEEN RABBIT

Original story by Margery Williams

Adapted by Ashley Crownover

Illustrated by Pat Thompson

There was once a beautiful Velveteen Rabbit. His coat was spotted brown and white, and his ears were lined with pink satin. On Christmas morning he was the most wonderful gift in the Boy's stocking. All morning, the Boy played with him. Then, in the excitement of looking at all the other presents, the Velveteen Rabbit was forgotten.

For a long time no one paid much attention to the Rabbit. The mechanical toys were rude to him because he was only a stuffed bunny. But the Play Horse, who had been there longer than any of the other toys—and knew all about toy magic—was very kind to the Rabbit.

One day the Rabbit asked the Play Horse, "What is Real? Does it mean having batteries or lights?"

"Real isn't how you are made," said the Play Horse. "It's a thing that happens to you. When a child really loves you, that is when you become Real."

One evening at bedtime, the Boy couldn't find the toy dog that slept with him, so his mother gave him the Rabbit instead. From then on, the Velveteen Rabbit slept with the Boy every night. The Boy would talk to him and they would play wonderful games—in whispers. The Rabbit slept snug and warm in the Boy's arms all night long.

Spring came, and wherever the Boy went, the Rabbit went, too. He had rides in the wheelbarrow and picnics on the grass. One day, he heard the Boy tell his mother, "My Bunny is Real. He's not a stuffed toy." That was the happiest day of the Rabbit's life.

After a while, the Velveteen Rabbit got raggedy from being loved so much. Some of his fur rubbed off and the pink in his ears turned gray, but the Boy didn't notice. He thought his Bunny was beautiful. When summer came, they played together in the woods almost every day.

Then one day, the Boy got very, very sick. The doctor said that all the toys in the room had to be tossed out because they were full of bad germs. The Boy got better, but the little Rabbit was put in a sack with other things and taken outside.

The Velveteen Rabbit wriggled his way to the top of the sack and looked out. Nearby he could see the woods where he and the Boy had played. He thought of how happy those times had been, and of how much the Boy had loved him. A tear trickled down his little shabby nose and fell to the ground.

Then a strange thing happened. Where the tear fell, a mysterious flower began to grow. It had emerald leaves and a beautiful golden blossom. The blossom opened and a fairy stepped out.

"I am the Toy Magic Fairy," she said. "I take care of the playthings that children have loved. When they are old and worn out, I make them Real."

"But wasn't I Real before?" the Rabbit asked.

The fairy said, "You were Real to the Boy because he loved you. Now you shall be Real to everyone."

In the meadow, the Velveteen Rabbit saw wild rabbits dancing with their shadows on the velvet grass.

"Run and play, little Rabbit," said the Toy Magic Fairy. "You are a Real Rabbit now."

Fall and winter passed. In the spring, when the days grew warm and sunny, the Boy went out to play. In the woods he saw two rabbits peeping at him from under a bush. One was gray. The other had brown and white spotted markings, a little soft nose, and bright round eyes that seemed familiar to the Boy.

"Why, he looks like my old Bunny who got lost when I was sick," the Boy thought.

He never knew that it really was his own Bunny, returning to look at the Boy who had first helped him to become Real.

*The End*